# waymaker

## FINDING THE WAY TO THE LIFE YOU'VE ALWAYS DREAMED OF

## STUDY GUIDE

### SIX SESSIONS

# BY ANN VOSKAMP

## WITH LISA-JO BAKER

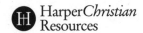

HarperChristian Resources

*WayMaker Study Guide*

© 2022 by Ann Morton Voskamp

Requests for information should be addressed to:
HarperChristian Resources, 3900 Sparks Dr. SE, Grand Rapids, Michigan 49546

ISBN 978-0-310-09077-9 (softcover)
ISBN 978-0-310-09078-6 (ebook)

HarperChristian Resources titles may be purchased in bulk for church, business, fundraising, or ministry use. For information, please e-mail ResourceSpecialist@ChurchSource.com.

Published in association with William K. Jensen Literary Agency, 119 Swanton Court, Eugene, Oregon 97404.

First Printing April 2022 / Printed in the United States of America

# Contents

# A Letter from Ann

Dear fellow pilgrim on The Way,

I have a gift for you as we begin this journey together. It's what we gave our eldest on the eve of his wedding. And I'd like nothing more than to slip it into your hand, too. It's a lifeline that's kept me from drowning more days than I can count.

Because, and let's be brutally honest here right from the start, life can often feel like walking out deep into a churning sea. Every day waves swell high around our necks and every night we've about had it up to our necks because we keep floundering through deep water and unexpected, upending news, diagnoses, relationships, and flat-out disappointments. And, yes you can say it out loud, the story of our lives, the expectations of our only life, haven't turned out to be quite what we always dreamed of.

So, today, wherever you are, whatever you are facing, that no one even knows or that you maybe haven't even put into words yet, in the very eye of your storm or at the bottom of your depths of disappointment or unspoken broken, **friend, can I give you my compass?**

A compass to find your way.

A compass to part the waves.

Because you and I are both pilgrims who each have to find our way—find The Way—to know God. Because pilgrimaging isn't just walking where Jesus walked, but walking *in the way* Jesus walked. And the spiritual practice that we're going to unpack in this study together is the soul's very real and directing compass to keeping company with God.

A decade ago, I began counting gifts as a daily habit to open my eyes to the real and active presence of God. I also scratch down the acronym **S.A.C.R.E.D. as a daily habit, a compass** that reorients me in relation to God.

This habit arises directly from Exodus 14—one of the most formational chapters of Scripture. God parts the waves before Moses and the people of Israel and shapes not only the identity of God's people then, but also foreshadows our deliverance now into a new way of being—and this way of life, this compass, offers a daily habit spelled out in just six letters.

In our time together, we'll dive into each letter and see how the WayMaker is not a far way off where you have to scream for His attention. He's no distracted lifeguard, oblivious while you flail and drown in the deep end. But instead, He is here, right here. He is right here in the way between your heartbeat and your next breath. It's when you give your whole self to the Way Himself that you know there's going to be a way through. He can be trusted. And you are going to make it. Because you, right now, are in the hands of the WayMaker.

Your fellow wayfarer,

# Introduction

## THE WAY AHEAD

As we begin this pilgrimage together, I hope you will prayerfully invite a group to go on the journey with you. Whether old friends or new, here is what to expect as we travel together:

## GROUP STUDY

- ✦ This guide contains six group study sessions to go with six video segments, each unpacking one of the SACRED habits that together teach us how to reorient our lives in relation to God.

- ✦ As you gather, you can expect your time together to include:

  - A **Welcome Letter from Ann** introducing the lesson you'll be studying together and what to be on the lookout for.

  - A chance to **Open Up** to one another.

  - Space to record **Video Notes and Reflections** from the segments.

  - An invitation to **Talk About It** with your group, interacting with the video lessons, the Bible, and your own stories.

  - A **Closing Prayer** to pray for one another.

# PERSONAL APPLICATION

In between each group study session, you are invited to a time of personal study and reflection. John Wesley, George Whitefield, Ignatius, King David, the apostle Paul—these fellow pilgrims—all made it a daily practice to examine their hearts, to scout out the topography of their souls, and locate themselves in relation to God. David said, "I have considered my ways and have turned my steps to your statutes" (Psalm 119:59). And Paul implored: "each one must examine his own work" (Galatians 6:4 NASB).

**Unless we make time for daily reflection, we can be making a road in the wrong direction.**

Use this time between sessions to reflect, to complete the study activities at your own pace, and to begin to journal using the SACRED compass prompts intended to put what you're learning into practice. Here is where we put on the daily habit of SACRED. Write it down like you're writing down directions. Because The Word is forging a Red Sea Road into more than finding a way through the waves, but also into a new way of being. A way of navigating daily closer to Christ.

SACRED journaling into Christ's sacred heart takes a handful of moments every morning that we can't afford to lose, since who can actually afford for their soul to lose its very way? And so, with Bible, pen, and journal in hand, we will locate our souls in relation to the WayMaker.

# STILLNESS
## to Know God

## GROUP STUDY

### WELCOME LETTER FROM ANN

*Please ask someone to read this letter aloud as you begin your time together:*

Welcome, friends!

Here we are at the beginning of a journey together. A pilgrimage if you will. Learning the habit of daily SACRED reorientation; finding ourselves in relation to God.

If I told you that life rarely lives up to the movies, I'm guessing I'd be preaching to the choir. Like you, I have a laundry list of disappointments where my plan for the life I dreamed of veered sharply and irrevocably away from my reality. I mean, who wants to admit that on their honeymoon they ended up sobbing in the shower when their just one-week-new husband wanted to leave their not-as-romantic-as-you-hoped-it-would-be getaway three days early to get back to the farm and his pigs?

And in the next two decades of marriage the waves would just keep coming. There would be plunging farm markets, and then skyrocketing debt, plummeting crop yields, and then steep, dizzying pig losses, kids who dropped out of school, out of college, out of our faith, mountain and valley, wave after wave after wave. And in seasons when the picture in my mind looked nothing like the reality staring back at me from the bathroom mirror, all I wanted to do was run away and demand answers from God.

So, let's start there. In session 1, those of us who are the frustrated, the disappointed, the irritated and the flat-out exasperated, let's get really honest about where we really are and what we really want. On my disappointing honeymoon, before we packed up and left, I walked down to the beach by myself and yelled at God across the lake: "Where are you?" I've yelled it many, many times since then.

It's a question you might be yelling right now, or aching with, or whispering when you lie in bed at night. A question straight out of Eden, like an echo of God's first recorded question to us: Where are *you*?

I want to invite you to listen to God's question. To think about how to answer God's question. To imagine God asking you with incredible attentiveness, winsome tenderness, and a deeply invested interest in your heart, your soul, your answer:

*Where are you?*

Your fellow pilgrim on The Way,

# OPEN UP

*Get to know who's on this pilgrimage with you. Group leader or volunteer, present the following question to the group for a brief time of opening up your time together.*

Where are you in your life right now? Briefly share what part of the story you're in: beginning, middle, plot twist, climax, stuck on repeat, lost on a detour? Take this opportunity to introduce the group to your stage in the life story.

# VIDEO NOTES AND REFLECTIONS

*View the video segment for Session 1. As you watch the video, use the following outline to note anything that stands out to you, any quotes you want to capture, and any questions or responses you may have.*

Stillness to know God. "Be Still and know God" (Psalm 46:10 paraphrase).

Stillness invites us to ask the question: What's in my way and what can I do about it?

Exodus 14

Our battle is to keep still—while God does the battle.

We are only seen and known as much as we are still.

EPS (or Expectational Positioning System) can steer us into disappointment at how our story has turned out.

*Ayekah* Hebrew: Where are you?

When we find the courage to be still and to be transparent, we find ourselves found.

God asks "Where are you in relation to Me?"

Be still because what's in the way is making a way. The obstacle is the miracle.

# TALK ABOUT IT

*Discuss as many of the following questions as you have time for. Ask for volunteers to read the Bible passages out loud. Invite robust conversation, every voice matters.*

1. What in the video moved you? Is there a quote or a story or an image that stuck most with you? Why?

2. Let's talk about EPS—our personal GPS that drives our lives. How has your own Expectational Positioning System gotten you lost and let you down?

3. Unpack the source of your expectations—where are all these untrustworthy directions coming from?

4. Read Genesis 3:8–10. Is it uncomfortable to think about God coming to find you? Why?

5. Describe how you picture the God who is asking you where you are? Is it strange to imagine Him as hurt? Why or why not?

6. Read Exodus 14. Honestly, unpack your reaction to the idea of being still. How would the group describe what this concept looks like in real life on a regular Wednesday, for example?

7. What kind of red sea are you facing in your own life right now? Write down what other members share so you can remember how to pray and support them in their story right now, too.

8. Can you remember what the S in the daily habit of SACRED stands for?

# CLOSING PRAYER

*Invite a group member to read the paragraphs below aloud. Then make time for everyone to share prayer requests. Close by bringing your prayers to the Father, either silently or out loud, as your group members feel most comfortable.*

Genuine prayer is having a genuine conversation with our Father; pull up a chair, lay your head, your heart, in His big, ole faithful hands. Prayer isn't giving God information to act upon, but God giving us intimacy to rest in. What undergirds every single prayer is the reality that we are held by our Father. As we go on this journey together, let's invite the Holy Spirit into our community and make room to hear where each person is really at. Prayer is a way to be still and invite God to act.

As you pray together, confess to God where you are in your life right now. Share the red sea you are facing. And invite Him to do as He promises, to fight for you while you remain still.

PRAYER REQUESTS

# PERSONAL APPLICATION

*Here is where we do the personal heart work. You and the WayMaker. Remember, new habits take time to learn. New rhythms require repetition. So, I suggest spreading out this personal study over several days between video sessions. And remember, this isn't about mindless repetition that feels like drudgery. Instead, this is like learning the lyrics to your favorite love song. A daily celebration of the songs the WayMaker sings over you.*

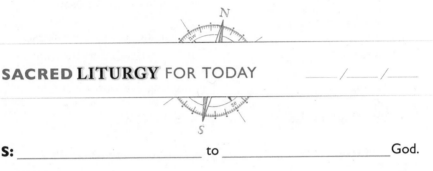

**SACRED LITURGY** FOR TODAY          ____/____/____

**S:** _____ to _____ God.

A liturgy is a sacred habit. Like a song stuck on repeat, it sings out loud and clear what we love. If we pay attention, our daily habits will reveal our truest romances. While our intentions might be good and true and beautiful, our habits are the real reflection of the heart we each wear on our sleeve.

A habit of turning to Facebook before opening the Word and facing His face, of being more consumed by the news than the Good News, of turning to Hollywood's stories to understand our own holy story instead of staying in His Story—and now we're wearing our real love on our sleeves.

Can you recognize your habits? Are you aware of the love songs playing on repeat in your life? Reflect on the list below. Honestly circle the life-draining habits you recognize from your own repetitive rhythms. Add any others you can think of.

Binging entertainment

Scrolling social media on a loop

Consuming constant news

Overeating

Purging

Punishing exercise

Negative self-talk

Gossiping

Nitpicking

Replaying painful conversations

Obsessing over the lives of others

Holding grudges

Mindless shopping

Constant comparison

Turning to alcohol, drugs, or pornography for comfort

Obsessive worry

Self-loathing

Trolling strangers online

Believing the worst of people

Exploding

Stuffing your emotions

Self-harm

_____

_____

_____

_____

_____

Our habits build what kind of life we inhabit. Our way of life is forming the way we are. And we may be shocked to discover that our faith-filled intentions are in misalignment with our actual behavior. And these habits, for better or for worse, are becoming our liturgies, our sacred habits. Because our daily way of life is the way we put on Christ—or not.

So, let us begin a new daily love liturgy with God. It always begins with your pen scratching down, letter by letter, a lifesaving compass for navigating your days, S.A.C.R.E.D.

**S** is the first letter in the SACRED Liturgy.

**S: <u>Stillness</u> to know God.** Write it out for yourself below:

**S:** _____ to _____ God.

What always comes first at the beginning of each day is being still, to know that He is still God. Stillness defiantly trusts: Because He is always with us.

Read Exodus 14:10–14. Underline the verbs.

Who is the subject of the verbs in this passage?

Did you notice how *God* is the subject of all the verbs in the story of the way through the red sea?

In the space that follows, reflect honestly on what you think about the idea of "Being Still." Is this a difficult concept for you to put into practice? Why or why not?

Charles Spurgeon said, "I dare say you will think it a very easy thing to stand still, but it is one of the postures which a Christian soldier learns not without years of teaching—'[Stillness] is one of the most difficult to learn under the Captain of our salvation. The Apostle Paul seems to hint at this difficulty when he says, 'Stand fast and having done all, still stand.'" Stillness may be the most difficult to learn, and to still stand.'"[1]

Stillness is an almost impossible posture in our culture that likes things fast, that reaches for the phone first before even turning on the light. We would rather keep forcing our own way forward, scrolling, trolling, stressing, obsessing, than stand still, when worry, uncertainty, fear or doubt, shame or failure are closing in.

Think about the last time you were truly still, in your heart and mind and soul. Picture and describe the circumstance or experience below. If you can't remember, then reflect instead on what is making your life feel so frantic?

Still hearts still see God. When there's no agitation of soul there can be a revelation of God. The only way to know what you're about is to so intimately know God, that you see yourself as God sees you.

# STILLNESS IS KNOWNNESS.

If it's true that our deepest desire is to be seen and known—then we are only seen and known as much as we are still. And we are only able to be still when we aren't being driven by our own expectations.

What are the expectations that are driving your agitation, your discontent, your life? Look each one in the eye and name them here:

In stillness:

Sanity is found. Sense is made of things. The roar of the enemy is stilled and the soul can listen to the whisper of its Maker.

You have to make time to be still—in order to make a life.

Write it down again. The first letter in our SACRED habit.

**S:** _____ to _____ God.

If stillness is knownness, it's worth considering:

## DO YOU REALLY WANT TO BE KNOWN BY GOD?

**Pause and consider the intimacy of that.** This is how David describes the experience:

"Search me, O God, and know my heart! Try me and know my thoughts! And see if there be any grievous way in me, and lead me in the way everlasting!"

### PSALM 139:23–24 ESV

We are used to asking God where HE is. Demanding answers from HIM. Inquiring as to HIS location. But do I really want to say where I am to I AM? Can you perhaps understand why Adam hid?

Read Genesis 3.

Dietrich Bonhoeffer retells the ancient story like so: "God speaks to Adam and halts him in his flight. Come out of your hiding place . . . out of your self-torment . . . Confess who you are, do not lose yourself in religious despair, be yourself. Adam, where are you?"[2]

This is the age of Adams—we evade the arms of God. Stay alone and you stay lost.

But when aloneness ends, lostness ends, and we have a God who names Himself the One who is with us.

It's striking that when God came to find Adam, He used the word *ayekah* when He could have used the more common, generic word for "where" in Hebrew, *eifoh*, which simply means to locate. *Eifoh* is the word Saul uses when seeking David, when Naomi asks about Ruth's whereabouts, when Joseph is trying to track down his brothers. *Ayekah*, on the other hand, expresses a heart motivation beyond mere location, and *ayekah* conveys expectations: "Where have you gone? Where are you if you are not here with me?"

When Adam and Eve turn away from intimacy with God—God cries *ayekah* because He's asking more than simply, "Where are you?" He's asking, "Where are you in relation to Me? Where have you gone that's taken you farther away from Me? Where are you when the expectation is that you and I would always be together?" God cries because there is distance between Him and His lover, and God's first known question of history asks you to orient to the topography of intimacy, to locate yourself in the Landscape of Love.

God knows what it's like for there to be trouble in paradise, for paradise to go all wrong, for the perfect way to fall away, for there to be distance. But for all the times nothing has turned out the way you dreamed and you've howled at God, "Where are you?", He's howled His own very first question of all time back to you, with that one word *ayekah* that sounds like:

"Where are you, when it was once all about you and Me—and now it's all about you and that damned lying snake? Woe is Me, where have you gone?

I just want you here with Me." For the Lord your God is looking for you, means to be "always with you. He celebrates and sings because of you…"

Write out Zephaniah 3:17. But don't write it here. Write it on a Post-it or a note card and stick it on your mirror. Or make it the background design on your phone's screen saver. Write it where you can see it daily.

The triune God isn't looking for you because He's disappointed in you. He isn't rebuking you, isn't rejecting you. The triune God delights in you, smiles over you, seeks to be with you, revives you with His kiss of grace, and can't stop singing love songs because of you. Right from the beginning, God has ached over any space and distance between us. When we were looking for a way out, God's woe over any distance between us drives Him to make a way to us. To be with us.

The cross points to the Way with open arms: Because our fall was detachment from God, our restoration is only found in attachment to God. If our first sin was to turn from God, detach the fruit from the tree, and savor it, then our return to wholeness is to turn, attach to God, and savor Him. Though our fall broke our attachment to God, He makes a way to us, slips His arms around us, and whispers all will be well now because He is Immanuel, God with us. Our story can only know restoration if our attachment to God is restored. The very symbol of the faith, the intersection of the cross, expresses how God purposes us for connection.

God has always been a WayMaker, making more than merely a way *through*. The WayMaker *is making a way to you.*

What if the only thing that will heal our hearts is to let Him fuse His own broken heart with ours? Now how do you feel about being searched out and known by God? Journal your thoughts and feelings below:

_____

_____

_____

_____

_____

_____

_____

_____

_____

_____

_____

_____

_____

_____

_____

_____

_____

_____

_____

## SACRED QUESTION FOR TODAY ____/____/____

## *"WHERE ARE YOU?"*

God's first recorded question in all of history, the very shortest question of the entire Hebrew Bible—Where are you?

Turn in your Bible to Genesis 3 and write out verse 9 below:

The most life-changing questions always are the shortest. In Hebrew we know it's only one word: *ayekah*. It's the question God has for you today and every day: *"Where are you?"*

Imagine your Creator walking in your garden or your apartment or to the back bedroom where you are hiding. Imagine Him calling to you by name—write your first name into the questions below and spend a few minutes answering in your most vulnerable and transparent voice:

Where are you, _____?

Where are you going with your life, _____?

Is this really where you want to be, _____?

Maybe your answer to that last question is, "No, I am not where I expected to be, not where I imagined I'd be, none of this is the way I thought it would be."

So very many saints all throughout history and Scripture have shared that sentiment:

- David had to keep putting one step in front of the other after being betrayed by his son Absalom.

- Martha had to find a way forward after Lazarus and all her hopes were bound in grave clothes and laid in the dark.

- Moses messed up at Meribah.

- Hagar had to find her way through when death stalked, dreams shattered, and she felt abandoned by all sense of hope.

But here's what I've learned, when an all-knowing God asks where you are, He isn't asking for your coordinates—He's asking you to seek out and coordinate your own heart with His.

He asks you where you are in your life because He wants you to name the place, see the circumstance, acknowledge the disillusionment and desperate hopes, to sit with it all—even *befriend* it.

What reaction do you have at the invitation to befriend where you are in your life right now? Circle all the feelings that apply:

| | | |
|---|---|---|
| Anger | Confusion | Disappointment |
| Revulsion | Fear | Delight |
| Disbelief | Anxiety | Surprise |
| Injustice | Relief | |

Spend a few moments writing one or two simple sentences about how sitting still in where you are in your life right now really feels.

Friend, *ayekah* means God understands everything going on inside you and doesn't want your soul to hide.

But what no one tells you is: When you hide who you are, what you ultimately are hiding from is yourself. This is a haunting, exhausting kind of lost. And if evil can keep you distracted from taking the time to ask your soul where you really are—he can take you every day farther from the life you envisioned.

When we find the courage to be still and to be transparent, we find ourselves found.

Only when you ask where you are every day—can you find your way. The God who asks where you are, He's large enough to hold you however, wherever you are.

Read Genesis chapter 22.

Unlike Adam, when Abraham heard God calling for him, Abraham answered *hineni* Hebrew.

Write Genesis 22:1 here to reflect on what a simple and straightforward answer *hineni* truly is:

*Hineni*: here.

Not in the sense of a roll call *here*, but in the sense of *I am all here*. Spoken only eight times in all of Scripture, every time *hineni* is the answer it is a transformative turning point.

## SACRED **APPLICATION** FOR TODAY ____ / ____ / ____

Friend, life is about location, location, location. So, no matter how brutally hard it is, unless we keep locating our soul—we'll keep losing our way.

Right now is a chance to quiet your soul, to stop striving or hiding, to let yourself be found in relation to where God is, right here. Be still and let God find you, like He found the Israelites on the edge of the Red Sea. The obstacle will be the miracle. Be still and be here, right here with God.

Take a deep breath. Look around.

What is in your way today? What are you trying to push past, to push down, to run away from? What is the obstacle in your way today? What is your Red Sea?

Now, in your stillness, what do you hear God saying in your heart? Listen, reflect, and write it below like a letter to yourself.

This can be an impression on your heart, a part of the teaching that deeply resonated with you, a revelation from a conversation you had with a friend, or a sense you have in your spirit as you come still and quiet before your Creator, trusting that He knows you. There is no wrong or right answer. Just practice being still and listening. Write down what you sense God saying about you and your obstacle today:

Dear _____,

I know you and I love you,
Jesus

# BONUS READING

As you reflect on what you have studied, learned, and journaled from Session 1 you may want to go deeper. Now is a good time to read chapters 1–4 of *WayMaker: Finding the Way to the Life You've Always Dreamed Of.*

# ATTENTIVENESS
## to Hear God

## GROUP STUDY

### WELCOME LETTER FROM ANN

*Please ask someone to read this letter aloud as you begin your time together:*

Dear Friends,

Today, wherever you are, whatever you are facing, together we are picking up the SACRED compass again. This compass that originates from the lessons learned by the people of Israel in Exodus 14 looks like a daily sacred habit to help you get your bearings whenever and wherever you feel lost. A compass that, like a liturgy, repeats and daily reroutes us closer and ever closer to God.

After completing Session 1, I hope your time of personal reflection and application helped you begin to unpack the question: Where are you? In your soul, in your heart, and in your mind. I hope you were able to tell God about the place in your life where you feel like you're between a rock and a hard place. And then I hope you were able to still… just pause to be still—and know that He is God, and He is on His throne, and you, right where you are, you are in His hands and He is here, as close as your next breath.

In our time together today, we will continue doing this holy work of seeing how each letter of our SACRED compass shows us the way to see how the WayMaker is not a far way off. But instead, how He is working through everything to do a new thing that we can trust even when we can't see it.

This is the SACRED way of life we are practicing:

**S:** <u>Stillness</u> to know God

**A:** <u>Attentiveness</u> to hear God

**C:** <u>Cruciformity</u> to surrender to God

**R:** <u>Revelation</u> to see God

**E:** <u>Examine</u> to return to God

**D:** <u>Doxology</u> to thank God

Attentiveness is the second letter in our SACRED habit—Attentiveness to hear God. Because attentiveness to what is happening *around* us is a way of being attentive to God *with* us.

I confess, at 16, I was paying attention to my awkwardness, my laced-up black leather orthopedic shoes, my horn-rimmed glasses. I was so busy paying attention to how lost I felt that I almost collided with the boy who would stun me by asking me on my first date.

Years later, I would be standing at a kitchen sink, suds up to elbows, and I would be thinking, I would be paying attention, to how being chosen is the dream. Because even when chosenness doesn't always mean you get your own way, what you get is the way of withness that destroys aloneness.

So, in our time together today, we will focus in and ask: What am I paying attention to? And, maybe even more significantly, who is the one who is paying attention to you?

Your fellow pilgrim on The Way,

## OPEN UP

*Get to know who's on this pilgrimage with you. Each week of group study will begin with a question for the whole group. Though not required, everyone is invited to respond.*

Share one thing that is pressing on your mind today? What is it that you can't stop circling back to over and over again this week? In short, what have you been paying the most attention to this week, spiraling back to whether you want to or not, consciously or unconsciously?

# VIDEO NOTES AND REFLECTIONS

*View the video segment for Session 2. As you watch the video, use the following outline to note anything that stands out to you, any quotes you want to capture, and any questions or responses you may have.*

Attentiveness to what is happening *around* us is a way of being attentive to God *with* us.

We become so used to asking questions *of* God, we drown out the questions God is *asking of us.*

God's questions:

Luke 9:20—"Who do you say I am?"

Genesis 16:8 ESV—"Where have you come from and where are you going?"

John 1:38—"What do you want?"

Where we focus our attention—determines our direction.

"It was not because you were more in number than any other people that the Lord set his love on you and chose you, for you were the fewest of all peoples, but it is because the Lord loves you" (Deuteronomy 7:7–8 ESV).

*Hesed:* entirely singular kind of love = You are chosen because God simply and forever chooses to perfectly attach Himself *to you.*

Realizing that God chooses you is the first step in paying attention to who God is.

We want things to go the way we choose—and God wants us to choose to trust His ways.

"Turn, Lord, and deliver me; save me because of your unfailing [*hesed-*attachment] love" (Psalm 6:4).

There is no pleasing God without trusting God (Hebrews 11:6).

# TALK ABOUT IT

*Discuss as many of the following questions as you have time for. Ask for volunteers to read the Bible passages out loud. Invite robust conversation, every voice matters.*

1. What in the video moved you? Is there a quote or a story or an image that stuck most with you? Why?

2. What are the questions you have been asking God lately? Take time to share one or two with the group.

3. How does it make you feel to imagine God sitting in the room, asking questions of *you*, and eager to hear your answers? Unpack your reactions. Why do you feel this way?

4. When was a time in your life you knew in the very marrow of your bones that you were chosen, wanted? Similarly, when did you feel *not* chosen, *un*wanted? Ask a few volunteers to share their stories.

5. Do you believe God when He says, "'Though the mountains be shaken and the hills be removed, yet my unfailing [*hesed*-love] for you will not be shaken nor my covenant of peace be removed,' says the LORD, who has compassion on you" (Isaiah 54:10). Why or why not?

6. Ask three people to each read a verse below and the question that God asks us. Share your responses as a group.

   Luke 9:20. Who do you say that God is?

   Genesis 16:8. Where are you coming from and where are you going?

   John 1:38. What do you want?

# CLOSING PRAYER

*Invite a group member to read the paragraphs below aloud. Then make time for everyone to share prayer requests. Close by bringing your prayers to the Father, either silently or out loud, as your group members feel most comfortable.*

Jesus knows turns you never heard of, makes roads you wouldn't have dreamed of, makes miracles happen exactly where you never would have imagined. There is a reason He is called the Way. There is more beyond what we can see, feel, imagine, and there is always dry land ahead. There is always a Red Sea Road coming to meet you. In unlikely ways. Waves may heave, but you have to believe: Love always finds His way to you.

### PRAYER REQUESTS

# PERSONAL APPLICATION

*Here is where we do the personal heart work. You and the WayMaker. Remember, new habits take time to learn. New rhythms require repetition. So, I suggest spreading out this personal study over several days between video sessions. And remember, this isn't about mindless repetition that feels like drudgery. Instead, this is like learning the lyrics to your favorite love song. A daily celebration of the songs the WayMaker sings over you.*

## SACRED **LITURGY** FOR TODAY          _____ / _____ / _____

We always begin by applying and practicing the SACRED habits we have learned so far. So, pick up your pen, friend, and start the day with a liturgy of love; reflect on the first letter and the first question in the acronym SACRED:

**S:** _____ to _____ God.

What is in my way today and what can I do about it?

The SACRED way of life has become my own rule of life and is literally what is making the way through my life! This is my prayer for you too, fellow pilgrim. That the spiritual discipline of SACRED is discipling the internal waves of worry and making a way to lean back and trust the wraparound presence of God holding you safe.

You can withstand life's rhythms of waves as long as you have your own interior sacred rhythms with God. The daily habit of a SACRED way of life holds back a storm of worries, a tsunami of fears, it sets the soul apart and lets the Spirit soothe the heart with gospel truth. Our soul's daily habits become our soul's eventual destination. Our SACRED spiritual disciplines keep turning our hearts to see, to arrive, in the arms of the WayMaker.

"Learning to love (God) takes practice."[3]

JAMES K.A. SMITH

So, open your journal, pick up your pen, and navigate closer to God as we study the second letter in our SACRED Liturgy.

**A: <u>Attentiveness</u> to hear God.** Write it out for yourself below:

**A:** _____ to _____ God.

I think we all suffer from some degree of Attention Deficit Disorder—a kind of soul ADD. And when we have attention deficit disorder with God, and we aren't living attentively to Him, it is our life that is at a deficit and we become deeply disoriented. In fact, with God-ADD, we become so used to asking questions *of* God, we drown out the questions God is *asking of us.*

As the people of Israel stand at the edge of the Red Sea, between the army of Pharaoh behind them and the vast and impassable sea before them, what does God say to them? Write out Exodus 14:15 below:

My heart pounded loudly as I studied this verse.

What you pay attention to is what you're spending your life on.

Pay attention to the problems, and you end up spending your one life on problems.

Pay attention to Love Himself, then you are spending your life on Love.

The reality is, we are selling our souls to whatever we are paying attention to.

Honestly journal what has your attention, right now, in this moment. It's likely a combination of all kinds of things.

_____

_____

_____

_____

_____

_____

_____

_____

_____

_____

_____

_____

_____

_____

_____

_____

_____

_____

_____

_____

_____

_____

_____

_____

_____

Take time to unpack where your attention is by writing down the five most pressing thoughts, weights, topics that your mind keeps circling back to over and over again in this moment. Boil them down to a single word each. Use the center of the target for the most pressing word and move outward, noting what is in your periphery.

⑤ _____

④ _____

③ _____

② _____

① _____

_____

This week the liturgy we are learning is to move from just listening to your own thoughts to listening to the WayMaker's ways. Can you do more than listen to your life, friend? Can you listen to your Lord? Because asking yourself the questions God asks you is how you start to find answers to the questions, worries, and weights you have written above. That is the habit of attentiveness we will unpack and practice this week.

## SACRED **STUDY** FOR TODAY ____ / ____ / ____

When I was eight, my mama walked into a psych ward and they locked the door behind her, and there was a wall between me and the first person who ever held me and loved me. If you're one of God's chosen, how come things you would never choose happen to you?

What is happening in your own life right now, friend, that you would never choose if it was up to you? Unburden yourself by writing some of it down here or in your journal.

Things *I Would Never Choose* that are happening right now to me and/or my people:

When you find yourself on a way you wouldn't choose, you've got to keep paying attention to the One who never stops paying attention to you, choosing you.

Realizing that God chooses you is the first step in paying attention to who God is.

Read Deuteronomy 7:7–8 and underline the words indicating how God feels about His people.

If you were reading in the original Hebrew, these are the words describing God's love that you would have read:

> "It was not because you were more . . . that the LORD set his
> [*hashaq*] love on you and chose you, for you were the fewest
> of all peoples, but it is because the LORD [*hesed*] loves you"
> (Deuteronomy 7:7–8 ESV).

Pay attention: No matter how hopeless you feel, or how abandoned you've felt, you were chosen because of *hesed* love.

In English, the word "lovingkindness" was invented in an attempt to translate the all-encompassing Hebrew word, *hesed*. But lovingkindness doesn't fully convey how *hesed* is an entirely different stratosphere of love. Used nearly 250 times in Scripture, in such a powerful manner that some theologians have suggested it may be the most important word in Scripture, *hesed* is the forever covenantal, always unconditionally, unwaveringly loyal, kind love of inseparable bonding, of divine family, of eternal attachment.

Pay attention: That's what *hesed*-love is: "*Hesed* is attachment love."

*Whatever rock and a hard place you find yourself in: Pay attention to a love like this.*

God chooses to love you simply because He chooses you to love > God wants to be with you because He wants to be with you > He *hesed*-loves you because He *hesed*-loves you.

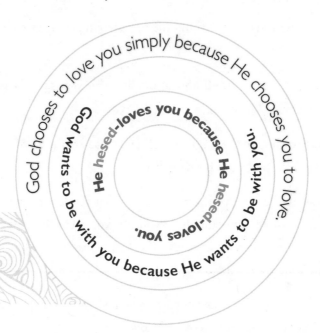

And this is the perfect circular logic of Love. You are captivating to the point that God bound Himself to you, making His heart captive to yours to liberate you from every lie that you are forsaken.

The lovingkindness of God is everywhere in everything—even if it doesn't show up in the kinds of ways you'd ever dreamed. Welcome to life, where Plan A transforms into Plan Z to transform *you*.

But maybe this points the way to a surrendered trust without borders in Him whose holy ways are higher than ours. We want things to go the way we choose—and God wants us to choose to trust His ways.

We expect more—and God expects us to trust Him more.

The ways God chooses for the chosen are ways that beg us to choose trust.

How do you choose to trust? Pay attention to Love Himself, pay attention to all the ways His *Hesed* is everywhere—shards of dawn's light splitting November dark, warm May rains on eyelashes, fireflies blinking like gathering stars all through the woods, your very name written into the veined hands of God—and you begin to trust Him in everything.

If God chooses to attach Himself to your soul, what can anyone say, or do, to shame you, to detach you from Love Himself? If God has covenanted lovingkindness to you, what crisis or catastrophe can ever break that kind of chosenness?

Read: Isaiah 54:10. *Hesed* shows up again in this verse.

> "'Though the mountains be shaken, and the hills be removed, yet my unfailing [*hesed*-love] for you will not be shaken nor my covenant of peace be removed,' says the LORD, who has compassion on you."

Rewrite this verse in your own words, putting your name and your current location and questions into the verse. Describe what you've learned about God through your stillness and waiting on Him.

I'll go first:

"Ann, though your family foundations be shaken and your dreams and hopes for your children be removed, yet my unfailing [*hesed*-love] for you, stronger than the Egyptian army, deeper than the Red Sea, more faithful than all the love stories this world has ever written will not be shaken nor my covenant of peace, my promise, my vow, my pledge, my word that is pure shalom be removed," says the Lord, who has compassion on me.

Your turn. Rewrite this verse with your own questions, worries, nagging fears, and let God's promise of unfailing *hesed*-love address those thoughts.

The assurance that you seek, the chosenness that you want, the grace that you crave, the hope that you need—it's there in His eyes tenderly and forever holding yours.

*Pay attention: Hesed* is who God is. And you are chosen not because of any of your choices, but because very God chooses you. And no choice you or anyone else makes has the power to make you unchosen. You are soul safe.

**SACRED QUESTION** FOR TODAY    \_\_\_\_ / \_\_\_\_ / \_\_\_\_

Now, you and I, as we practice our SACRED question, we need to do more than just listen to our lives—we need to listen to our Lord. Attentiveness leads to receptiveness. And the more attentive we are to what is happening in our lives, the more receptive we are to seeing the WayMaker and His *hesed*-lovingkindness at work.

How often have you questioned God—but never answered God's questions of you? Isn't God asking questions of us all the time?

Maybe if we begin to attend to, to answer God's questions, we'd be less likely to question God's ways? Maybe asking yourself the questions God asks you starts to give you answers?

Look up these three verses, and fill in the questions God asks as well as your answers:

| | WHAT QUESTIONS DOES GOD ASK IN THESE PASSAGES? | WHAT IS YOUR ANSWER? |
|---|---|---|
| **Luke 9:20** | | |
| **Genesis 16:8** | | |
| **John 1:38** | | |

## SACRED APPLICATION FOR TODAY _____/_____/_____

The **A** of attentiveness is paying attention, the second daily habit that, like a compass, will orient you when you are lost. When we are attentive to God, we *hear* Him.

"What you pay attention to, is what you will remember, and what you remember is what you will anticipate in the future"?[4]

### CURT THOMPSON, *ANATOMY OF THE SOUL*

Pay attention to *hesed*-lovingkindness everywhere, and you will remember it, and anticipate *hesed*-lovingkindness coming to meet you with arms wide-open tomorrow. When you keep paying attention to God's questions of the soul, God's own questions in Scripture, you are paying attention to Love Himself beckoning you:

> *Who do you say that I am?*
> *Where are you coming from and where are you going to?*
> *What do you want?*

So when you feel like you've driven off the edge of the map, when you've lost your sense of direction and it feels like you're losing your senses, when you can't imagine making sense of your story because your story took an unexpected turn, then it's time, friend, simply be still (S)… and know that

He is God. Then, stop paying attention to what's in the way, and start paying attention to the One who is paying attention to you (A).

It's time to pick up your pen and be still and genuinely attentive to God's first and perhaps most important question "Where are you?"—Genesis 3:9. Journal through your answer below:

_____

_____

_____

_____

_____

_____

_____

_____

_____

_____

_____

_____

_____

_____

_____

_____

_____

_____

_____

_____

_____

Attend to God's questions to tend your own soul. Attending to where you are tends to change the *way* you are. Be attentive to hear God.

## BONUS READING

As you reflect on what you have studied, learned, and journaled from Session 2, you may want to go deeper. Now is a good time to read chapters 5–8 of *WayMaker: Finding the Way to the Life You've Always Dreamed Of.*

# CRUCIFORMITY
## to Surrender to God

## GROUP STUDY

### WELCOME LETTER FROM ANN

*Please ask someone to read this letter aloud as you begin your time together:*

Friends,

Where are you at today? More than where are your feet at—but where is your soul at? Is your soul discouraged and downcast? Or finding its way through to an expansive and welcoming place?

Wherever you are, remember that the God who creates something out of nothing can create exoduses through anything. The God who raises the dead can raise any dead dreams, and he can move by any means. Hope isn't insisting on the way we imagined things would go, but having an imagination that whatever comes our way will be worked out *for our good*.

The one miracle you can always count on, like forty years of manna in the desert, is the sustaining withness of God. Without fail. With God, hope is always justifiable. God will slice an ocean of waves in half to find a way to be with you.

Where there seems to be no way—is exactly the way to miracles.

This SACRED liturgy we're learning together opens our eyes to the ways the WayMaker is always working:

> **S:** <u>Stillness</u> to know God. **What always comes first is being still, to know that He is still God.**

> **A:** <u>Attentiveness</u> to hear God. **Paying attention to the three questions God asks us.**

*Who do you say that I am?* I say that You are—Abba. Father. Chin-lifter. Wound Binder. WAYMAKER.

*Where am I coming from and where am I going to?* If I want a real living relationship with God—I need to pay attention to where my soul is in relationship to God. What distance, what apathy, what distractions, what anxiety am I coming from… and what focus, what intentionality, what attention, what peace, what Love am I going to?

*What do I want?* Jesus really asks that question, both in John 1 and Mark 10: What do you want? He's really asking you—what do you want? Do I want to be distressed, anxious, bothered— what do they help me gain? There is always something to be worked up about, if you want. But the reality is that God is always at work, and there is always something to be thankful for, which is what makes you joyful, if you want.

And today we turn to the letter "C" in the word SACRED, the letter in the center of SACRED and the crux of absolutely everything—Cruciformity—to surrender to God.

Your fellow pilgrim on The Way,

## OPEN UP

*Get to know who's on this pilgrimage with you. Each week of group study will begin with a question for the whole group. Though not required, everyone is invited to respond.*

When was the last time you were required to make a truly sacrificial gesture? Can you describe it? And share how it made you feel?

# VIDEO NOTES AND REFLECTIONS

*View the video segment for Session 3. As you watch the video, use the following outline to note anything that stands out to you, any quotes you want to capture, and any questions or responses you may have.*

Cruciformity to surrender to God. This is the crux of everything.

*God said to Moses*: "Raise your staff and stretch out your hand over the sea to divide the water so that the Israelites can go through the sea on dry ground" (Exodus 14:16).

Jesus is the new and better Moses in cruciform surrender to the will and way of God.

What do I need to surrender today?

Sacrifice—is an expression of connection and communion.

Sacrifice, *korban*, comes from the Hebrew root, K-R-V, which literally means to come near, an approach, a moving closer, to move into a closer relationship.

Hannah prayed a *korban* prayer.

Cruciformity is about vulnerability, which leads to intimacy, which leads to everything we've ever wanted or dreamed of.

Cruciformity is always what transforms.

# TALK ABOUT IT

*Discuss as many of the following questions as you have time for. Ask for volunteers to read the Bible passages out loud. Invite robust conversation, every voice matters.*

1. What in the video moved you? Is there a quote or a story or an image that stuck most with you? Why?

2. Who does Moses embody standing at the edge of the Red Sea, in Exodus 14:16?

3. Unpack this statement as a group, "The life of Jesus is an exodus, hidden in plain sight."

4. How did Ann's guide through Israel define the word *sacrifice*?

5. Why did Hannah ask God to make a way to a child—and then give back the very dream child the WayMaker made a way to?

6. If sacrifice is not losing something but moving closer to someone, how does that change how you understand the story you are currently in the middle of?

7. Ask a few people if they're willing to share an example when: Trying to self-protect their dreams led to self-destruction.

8. Ask a few volunteers to share what they need to surrender in order to live cruciform.

## CLOSING PRAYER

*Invite a group member to read the paragraphs below aloud. Then make time for everyone to share prayer requests. Close by bringing your prayers to the Father, either silently or out loud, as your group members feel most comfortable.*

Your story may seem to make no sense, but the WayMaker is working all the lines into a way through it all, to be in sacred union with you. Even when you can't see that He's doing *SACRED* work, He's working to part waters to set you apart for a deeper communion with Himself. The WayMaker never, ever, ever, ever stops making a way to be closer to you.

──────── PRAYER REQUESTS ────────

# PERSONAL APPLICATION

*Here is where we do the personal heart work. You and the WayMaker. Remember, new habits take time to learn. New rhythms require repetition. So, I suggest spreading out this personal study over several days between video sessions. And remember, this isn't about mindless repetition that feels like drudgery. Instead, this is like learning the lyrics to your favorite love song. A daily celebration of the songs the WayMaker sings over you.*

## SACRED **LITURGY** FOR TODAY          ____ / ____ / ____

We always begin by applying and practicing the SACRED habits we have learned thus far. So, pick up your pen, friend, and start the day with a liturgy of love; reflect on the first two letters in the acronym SACRED and journal your answers below:

**S:** _____ to _____ God.

What is in my way today and what can I do about it?

**A:** _____ to _____God.

Who do I say that God is?

Where am I coming from and where am I going to?

What do I want?

C is the third letter, the third step, in a daily habit that, like a compass, will orient you when you are lost.

**C:** <u>Cruciformity</u> **to surrender to God.** Write it out for yourself below:

**C:** _____ to _____God.

What exactly *is* cruciformity?

To be cruciform is to be shaped and formed like a cross. To be cruciform is the essence of what it means to be shaped and formed into the image of Christ. Cruciformity is what we see Moses embodying at the edge of the Red Sea, when he's caught between a rock and a hard place.

**Read and write out what God said to Moses in Exodus 14:16.**

If Moses was a type of Christ, who stretched out his hand over the sea to divide the water so that the Israelites could go through on dry ground, and if Jesus is the new and better Moses—then didn't both of their exoduses down Red Sea Roads begin with hands raised, arms stretched out, in cruciform surrender to the will and way of God?

A cross-shaped life is an exodus-shaped life[5]: In Christ, there is always a way through. What if the question is never "What's the way *out* of this?" but "What way can I be *in* this?" The way through happens when we stop focusing on how to get out of something and focus on what we can get out of this to become Christlike.

Consider where you are in your story today, standing facing your Red Sea. Can you raise your arms in surrender to Christ, vulnerably outstretched, palms wide-open like the vertical beam of the cross, arms reaching upward to Christ? Journal how you can be in this and how you can become more Christlike out of this.

Now, consider the horizontal beam of the cross, arms reaching outward, from you to others. Because the way to happiness is always to bless and bless and bless, by caring and curving toward other people's needs. How is the story you can't get out of giving you a way to move closer in, connect with, care for, and bless others?

Cruciformity is the shape and form of attachment, arms outstretched upward to God and outward to people, and *cruciformity* is always what *transforms*.

## SACRED **STUDY** FOR TODAY    : _____ / _____ / _____

Several years ago, I landed in Israel to spend a one-week pilgrimage literally walking the way through John 2 to John 21, following the sacred way of Jesus. Our guide pointed toward this rocky outcropping, to where holes were found carved into rocks, perhaps the very postholes that once supported the tabernacle itself. Our guide said, "After the Israelites came across the Red Sea, wandered forty years in the wilderness, and finally entered the promised land, the entire nation of Israel made its way here to Shiloh to make their sacrifices to God."

"Now, when the tabernacle was right here," the guide held up two fingers, "you could have come here with two different kinds of sacrifices: the *olah* sacrifice, a sacrifice that is completely consumed in flame before God. Or you could come here to Shiloh with the *shelamim* sacrifice—which comes from the word *shalom*—the peace offering."

Shalom? I'm thinking. A shalom sacrifice? Here at Shiloh? Did the WayMaker lead this mother of one girl named Shalom, desperately trying to adopt another girl we've fallen in love with and would name Shiloh Shalom, into this wilderness to speak a holy word—to sacrifice and lay down every one of her dreams? I stepped in closer and tried to memorize the guide's words that came next.

"And this peace sacrifice, it is actually eaten by those who sacrifice it, almost like a shared meal, almost like a feast between man and God, almost like a communion—an expression of connection."

Wait, I'm thinking. Sacrifice—is an expression of connection?

Sacrifice—is a way of communion?

My entire theology of sacrifice was suddenly tripping all over itself.

How about you? What comes to mind when you hear the word *sacrifice?*

"Wait—," I interrupted the guide, before he moved on. "Sacrifice—doesn't mean give up or lay down or go without or let go of?"

"No, no, no," he said . . . "Sacrifice doesn't mean that at all."

Standing on the site of the Tabernacle of God, our Messianic Jewish guide showed us, from the text, that sacrifice in Hebrew is *korban*. The guide flipped the pages of his worn Bible to show me. "See?" he says, "Sacrifice, *korban*, comes from the Hebrew root, K-R-V, which literally means to come near, an approach, a moving closer, to move into a closer relationship."

**Sacrifice is not losing something but moving closer to Someone.**

**Sacrifice isn't about loss—sacrifice is about love.**

**Sacrifice is about detaching from one thing—to attach to a greater thing.**

Now what comes to mind when you hear the word *sacrifice*?

## SACRED **QUESTION** FOR TODAY _____ / _____ / _____

To practically figure out what it means to live a cross-shaped life to know an exodus-shaped way through life, we need to begin by asking, What do I need to surrender today?

What do I need to surrender in one hand, so I can reach out to God . . . and to people . . . and live given, live vulnerable, live cruciform?

Consider below what that looks like for you today:

| WHAT DO I NEED TO SURRENDER TODAY? | HOW DOES THAT FREE UP MY HANDS TO CONNECT WITH GOD? | HOW DOES THAT FREE UP MY HANDS TO CONNECT WITH PEOPLE? |
| --- | --- | --- |
| | | |

If you live the cruciformity of vulnerability—of letting go—you find the way to what your soul really wants most: **intimacy**.

Because surrender isn't about loss—it's about love. Sacrifice isn't about loss—sacrifice is about connection, sacrifice is about intimacy. Lay down your *korban*, to be lifted up into what you really want: connection. Make your dream into a *korban*—and you get the dream of moving closer to God—and you can't move closer to God, to hold on to more of Him.

Trying to self-protect our dreams—can be how we self-destruct.

Recall how we tracked that a habit initially meant what you wear, like a nun wears a habit? The way to a new way of being, to a new habit, is to focus first on your new identity. You can set goals to change the way you are, the way things are—like, I am going to run 5K every day… but that habit doesn't become your way of life until you take on a new identity: I am a runner. And similarly—in Christ? Cruciform is the form of your new identity, the form of your never-failing security, the form of your needed serenity.

So track with me here: In Christ, because of Christ at the cross, Cruciformity is your SACRED identity—which shows you the way to vulnerability—which makes a way to what your soul longs for, dreams of most: intimacy.

**Wherever you are right now . . .**
**say it out loud like a reorienting to your soul:**

**"Cruciformity is always what transforms."**

Then write it out like a student writing lines for their teacher. Over and over, big or small, colored in, print or cursive. Think to yourself as you write, *I am conforming to the cross, to Christ crucified.* Fill up the whole space below with these words:

**Cruciformity is always what transforms.**

# SACRED **APPLICATION** FOR TODAY ____/____/_._

Cruciformity is about vulnerability, which leads to intimacy, which leads to everything we've ever wanted or dreamed of. To form your life into the shape of a cross is to live with your arms stretched wide-open, conforming to the crucified life of Christ.

We reach out to God and to people and relentlessly talk back to every worry with the cruciform prayer the crucified WayMaker prayed in the garden: *Into Your hands, Lord, I commit this. Commit this fear, this person, this worry, this situation. I surrender to You my sins, my people, my dreams, my tomorrows. Surrendering all of me, reaching out to people, reaching out to You.*

**So, pick up your pen, and ask yourself:**

What do I need to surrender today so I can live cruciform . . . to transform the way of my whole life?

# BONUS READING

As you reflect on what you have studied, learned, and journaled from Session 3, you may want to go deeper. Now is a good time to read chapters 9–11 of *WayMaker: Finding the Way to the Life You've Always Dreamed Of.*

# REVELATION
## to See God

## GROUP STUDY

## WELCOME LETTER FROM ANN

*Please ask someone to read this letter aloud as you begin your time together:*

Fellow pilgrims,

It's a new day and a new opportunity to locate ourselves in relation to the WayMaker who is always making the best way forward for us. *You and I, dear friends, we are not staying where we are today; we are on the way.* Thomas Aquinas described the core identity of human beings as "homo viator,"[6] pilgrims on the journey, humans on the way.

You and I are pilgrims, not staying here in this place, in your head, in your relationships, in your thinking, in your understanding, in your marriage, in your self-orientation, in your relation to God.

I trust you have pen and notebook and compass in hand, because if we have a living relationship with God—we need to keep locating where our soul is in relation to God. So, let's begin again with our SACRED way of life that is showing us the way through. Let's ask ourselves the questions we've been practicing daily based on our faithful compass, the acronym SACRED:

**S:** <u>Stillness</u> to know God. **What is in your way today?**

**A:** <u>Attentiveness</u> to hear God. **Who do you say that God is today? Where are you coming from and where are you going to? And what do you want?**

**C:** <u>Cruciformity</u> to surrender to God. **What do you need to surrender today?**

**R:** And now we turn to the letter "R" in the word SACRED. R for **<u>Revelation</u> to see God.**

May He give us the eyes to see His blazing light even in our darkest nights.

Your fellow pilgrim on The Way,

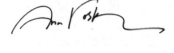

# OPEN UP

*Get to know who's on this pilgrimage with you. Each week of group study will begin with a question for the whole group. Though not required, everyone is invited to respond.*

Describe a time in your life, maybe it's right now, when your journey seemed shrouded in darkness, the way forward impossible to see.

# VIDEO NOTES AND REFLECTIONS

*View the video segment for Session 4. As you watch the video, use the following outline to note anything that stands out to you, any quotes you want to capture, and any questions or responses you may have.*

**R** is the fourth letter in our SACRED habit—Revelation to see God.

Exodus 14:19–20

Terrible clouds can be torches.

Romans 8:14. A cloud-fire guide then and the Holy Spirit as a Guide now.

Mystery holds revelation.

Not asking for eyes to see God IN the darkness, we become blind and lost and afraid.

Augustine of Hippo named our human tendency to want to self-soothe:

*homo incurvatus in se*—every human turned and curved inward toward self.

All addictions are wrong attachment, and the cure to all addiction is a right attachment.

The way out of pain is to reach out, cruciform.

The prodigal has a plan to negotiate—but the father has a plan to extricate, reinstate, and celebrate the prodigal.

Trying to self-protect is how you begin to self-destruct.

# TALK ABOUT IT

*Discuss as many of the following questions as you have time for. Ask for volunteers to read the Bible passages out loud. Invite robust conversation, every voice matters.*

1. What in the video moved you? Is there a quote or a story or an image that stuck most with you? Why?

2. Have you considered how long the Israelites were trapped between the Red Sea and the Egyptian army, through both daylight and nighttime hours in Exodus 14:19–20?

3. Unpack this statement as a group, "Mystery holds revelation."

4. Describe a time in your life when you were looking for a sign from God? Did you see it? How was it revealed?

5. What is the cloud that goes before us, lighting the way for us today?

6. What is the one real danger that lurks in the dark for pilgrims on the way? How can we help one another in the dark? How do we, ourselves remain drawn to the light?

7. Unpack the dangers of our human tendency to want to curve inward toward self, what Augustine described as *incurvatus in se*, self-soothing, and how they can lead to addiction.

8. Ask a few volunteers to share a time when the darkness they were journeying through led to an apocalyptic, momentous, or catastrophic revelation from God. Describe the darkness and the difference God revealed.

## CLOSING PRAYER

*Invite a group member to read the paragraphs below aloud. Then make time for everyone to share prayer requests. Close by bringing your prayers to the Father, either silently or out loud, as your group members feel most comfortable.*

Could anything be more insulting than shrinking back from your beloved's outstretched hand and murmuring, "I don't trust you. I don't trust you to love me, I don't trust you to take care of me, I don't trust you to have my best interests at heart, I don't trust you to be there for me, I don't trust you to bring me into any promised land, I don't trust your ways at all. I'll cling to my comfort of choice instead."

Friends, God aches to comfort you. God runs to meet you. God will cover your shame with His love. He is a good God Father and His love holds. Ask Him to give you the eyes to see Him in your darkness. He is already there.

PRAYER REQUESTS

# PERSONAL APPLICATION

*Here is where we do the personal heart work. You and the WayMaker. Remember, new habits take time to learn. New rhythms require repetition. So, I suggest spreading out this personal study over several days between video sessions. And remember, this isn't about mindless repetition that feels like drudgery. Instead, this is like learning the lyrics to your favorite love song. A daily celebration of the songs the WayMaker sings over you.*

## SACRED **LITURGY** FOR TODAY        ____ / ____ / ____

We always begin by applying and practicing the SACRED habits we have learned thus far. So, pick up your pen, friend, and start the day with a liturgy of love; reflect on the first three letters in the acronym SACRED and journal your answers below:

**S:** _____ to _____God.

What is in my way today and what can I do about it?

**A:** _____ to _____God.

Who do I say that God is?

Where am I coming from and where am I going to?

What do I want?

**C:** _____ to _____God.

What do I need to surrender today?

And now we turn to the letter "R" in the word SACRED.

**R: Revelation to see God.** Write it out for yourself below:

**R:** _____ to _____ God.

Revelation is the fourth letter in our SACRED habit—Revelation to see God. And, if we're being soul honest here, then what we're really asking is to be able to see God in the dark, in the valley, in the shadow of death. Eyes to see how the darkness itself reveals God, the SACRED revelatory Light in the dark.

In Exodus as the people of Israel stood between the seemingly immovable rock of the Red Sea in front of them and the hard, terrible place of the entire Egyptian army behind them, this is what they saw in the dark:

> Then the angel of God who was going before the host of Israel moved and went behind them, and the pillar of cloud moved from before them and stood behind them, coming between the host of Egypt and the host of Israel. And there was the cloud and the darkness. And it lit up the night without one coming near the other all night (Exodus 14:19–20 ESV).

Please write out that last astonishing sentence here:

The cloud—lit up the night . . . a cloud that's fire in the night? Who would've ever imagined that? A shroud of cloud with a flaming blaze at its center.

How did the book of Nehemiah describe it? Write Nehemiah 9:12 below:

Fellow pilgrim, wayfarer on the Way, this is how we begin to see like we've never seen before, this is how we start to see in the dark:

What's clouded in mystery is also a flame to light the way.

The cloud over you is also the light before you. Clouds can be light. Which is another way of testifying:

What is in the way—is making the way.

And I know there will be days when you think this a mocking joke, that any of these dark clouds could be lighting the way, and you will weep, but there will be days when you know it and will not be afraid:

Terrible clouds can be torches.

Within the clouds—there is a light to lead the way.

Mystery holds revelation.

Write out this week's SACRED letter again for orientation.

**R:** _____ to _____God.

Can you reframe whatever you're up against as a cloud on fire? Can you identify the revelation in the midst of your darkness and mystery? Take five to ten minutes to chew on this idea. Sit quietly and repeat the phrases above over and over in your mind . Write them out, journal about what they signify for you, or draw a picture—whatever works best for you to let this new way of seeing soak in.

_____

_____

_____

_____

_____

_____

_____

_____

_____

_____

_____

_____

_____

_____

_____

I don't know what hope or dream you are quietly carrying right now in a corner of your heart and I don't know if you're looking for a sign like the Israelites were looking for a sign, but if they ever needed a sign that God was with them, that the WayMaker was making a way, this was it: a cloud on fire.

I know we'd prefer some banner slung behind a low-flying plane, a note in all caps from God flapping in the wind. Or a flourishly-scrawled letter, handwritten by the Divine with gilded ink and postmarked from the pearly gates and slipped directly through the mail slot like an angel feather drifting to our feet. Or how about a neon flashing marquee in the night, blinking like a warning on the cosmic dashboard: THIS IS THE WAY.

But isn't the Word, this Spirit-inspired book, a sign for all time now, a certain revelation of God now? Because God wants to be known by us, He communicates with us through His Word, and He communicates through creation around us, through our conscience in us, through Christ with us even now. All the world's a seashell and if you lift it up, and really listen, you can hear the ocean of God.

God still speaks, friend.

And, like the pillar of cloud-fire once led, the presence of the Spirit-fire leads now. Like God gave the children of Israel a cloud-fire guide—He gives His children now the Holy Spirit as a Guide. Look it up and write it down:

| HOW THE SPIRIT LED THE PEOPLE OF ISRAEL EXODUS 13:21 | HOW THE SPIRIT LEADS US TODAY ROMANS 8:14 |
|---|---|
|  |  |

Friend, you have your own cloud aflame and it is the comfort of the Holy Spirit. You have your own Holy Ghost to lead you through the thick dark.

You have a Mystery, to lead you through your mysteries.

*Mystery holds revelation.*

## SACRED **STUDY** FOR TODAY          ____ / ____ / ____

Honestly? When we aren't asking for eyes to see God IN the darkness, to catch that fiery revelation in the midst of our darkest nights, we can become blind and lost and afraid. Ask me how I know.

I have walked dark valleys, I have been the prodigal, I have chosen everything over my Father God and I have been pig-pen low, and valley-of-the-shadow-of-death desperate. I have suffered literal physical heart failure and at the same time it has felt like my soul flatlined and I haven't been able to see in the dark.

There was a time when our youngest son, a Type 1 diabetic, had a blood sugar low that sucked him into eye-rolling seizures, then limp unconsciousness, and we were bent under the white lights of the ER praying for our kid to live. We drove another child to the city hospital to have a thyroid radiated and embarked on this daily and relentless calibration of meds for Graves' disease and having a manual thyroid for life. And we've paced long hospital hallways while our youngest had her chest cut open, not once but twice, as her heart went under the knife.

Then, the way life unexpectedly, constantly turns: One of our kids dropped out of high school—and another dropped out of university—and another dropped out of church and comes and tells me they don't want to come to Jesus anymore. And sometimes the dark is so dark, we can forget what the light looks like.

Life in the dark is trying to hold our heads up to breathe through the crashing waves. And the only real danger is to stop moving in the way. To quit being *in via*, on the way, and instead, to start curving away from the WayMaker and toward ourselves. To let the darkness and the fear and the loneliness and the worry and the hurt and the heartbreak and the shame disorient us so that instead of looking for revelation in the dark, we start looking for relief.

Write down some of the things lurking in your dark today:

Augustine of Hippo named our human tendency to want to self-soothe. He called us *homo incurvatus in se*—every human turned and curved inward toward self.[7] This curving toward self-sufficiency, self-protection, self-comfort, self-interest is the bent way of being human. We're wired for attachment, for dependence on God, but our inclination toward *incurvatus in se* turns the direction of our dependence toward destructive things, and our attachments go awry. Instead of seeking a revelation from God—we seek relief from anything else.

And when we start seeking some quick relief more than God-revelation, we can get lost in a long addiction.

All addiction is an attachment in the wrong direction.

Can you be honest enough with yourself today to name the ways you self-soothe? Name the ways your own *incurvatus in se* is curving and bending your own heart right here and now.

Write down some of the ways you self-soothe instead of Spirit-soothe here:

You've just named your addiction(s). I know that can sound hard, harsh even, but it's a warning. It's an alarm bell clanging wildly, and we have GOT to pay attention.

We are given a clanging alarm ringing out loud and clear in Scripture. Look up Proverbs 14:12–13 in a few different translations if you can and write them out below:

It's even more jarring in The Message version: "There's a way of life that looks harmless enough; look again—it leads straight to hell."

And maybe the bruised and battered and better explanation for why we crave comfort is this: At the heart of all addiction is a broken attachment that leaves a broken heart.

The food addict, the screen addict, the game addict, the pill addict, the bottle addict, the porn addict, the gambling addict, the person addict, the shopping addict, the comfort addict—all addicts carry a hurt in the wrong direction, looking for a way out of pain. A way out of the dark, around the dark, past the dark. When we can't conceive of walking *through* the dark with our own Cloud Fire of the Holy Spirit Himself, we are in bondage. All addictions are wrong attachment, and the cure to all addiction is a right attachment.

Reflect on the lists you just wrote. What does it look like for you to move through your pain and your dark from *bondage from God* to *bonding with God*, friend?

| I AM IN PAIN IN THESE PLACES | I AM IN SELF-SOOTHING BONDAGE IN THESE PLACES | I AM INVITED INTO BONDING WITH GOD IN THESE PLACES |
|---|---|---|
| DARKNESS OR PAIN | SELF-SOOTHING SOLUTION | HOW I CAN BOND WITH GOD IN RIGHT ATTACHMENTS |
| For example: My marriage is in trauma. | I am binging and purging. | I can fill myself with God's promises of love. I can look for God's blazing torch of *hesed*-love. The cross is the seal of my marital union with God, He will always be my first and last love. His promise burns like a torch in the darkness:<br><br>Therefore, behold, I will allure her,<br>    and bring her into the<br>        wilderness,<br>    and speak tenderly to her.<br>And there I will give her her<br>        vineyards<br>    and make the Valley of Achor<br>        a door of hope.<br>And there she shall answer as in<br>        the days of her youth,<br>    as at the time when she came<br>    out of the land of Egypt.<br><br>(Hosea 2:14–15 ESV). |

| I AM IN PAIN IN THESE PLACES | I AM IN SELF-SOOTHING BONDAGE IN THESE PLACES | I AM INVITED INTO BONDING WITH GOD IN THESE PLACES |
|---|---|---|
| DARKNESS OR PAIN | SELF-SOOTHING SOLUTION | HOW I CAN BOND WITH GOD IN RIGHT ATTACHMENTS |
| My prodigal child has cut us off. | I am mindlessly scrolling social media for hours. | Deserts are places of dependence on God. Deserts are not places where God deserts me, but places I hear from God. Every wilderness holds God's tenderness, and the driest of deserts can be the holy of holies. Deserts aren't places to fear: Deserts are trust greenhouses. Desperation can always be a door. I choose to still and attentively listen to the ways He is working, moving, wooing. |
| My family is going through a death. | I am trying to escape my pain through alcohol or pornography or drugs. | This pain is leading me, reminding me that The WayMaker works in ways far higher and kinder than my choices right now. God never stops working to take care of me in ways that are working more good than I ever dream. Now is my chance to trust God with this pain, not to deflect from it. But to let it open me to more of His loving-kindness. "With God on our side like this, how can we lose? If God didn't hesitate to put everything on the line for us, embracing our condition and exposing himself to the worst by sending his own Son, is there anything else he wouldn't gladly and freely do for us?" (Romans 8:31–32 MSG). |

Now it's your turn, friend.

| I AM IN PAIN IN THESE PLACES | I AM IN SELF-SOOTHING BONDAGE IN THESE PLACES | I AM INVITED INTO BONDING WITH GOD IN THESE PLACES |
|---|---|---|
| MY DARKNESS OR PAIN | MY SELF-SOOTHING SOLUTION | HOW I CAN BOND WITH GOD IN RIGHT ATTACHMENTS |
|  |  |  |
|  |  |  |
|  |  |  |
|  |  |  |
|  |  |  |

Once you've worked through most of the items on your lists, know that you have begun the vital work of reorienting your daily habits, your sacred loves, back toward God. This is how you transfer your trust and attachments back to God, the only Way through your pain, the only Light to lead the way.

## SACRED QUESTION FOR TODAY ___/___/___

Unless we long for more of a revelation of Love Himself —we fall into addictions to far lesser loves, that make us far lesser versions of ourselves. We are all the broken-hearted prodigal of Luke desperate to find a way out of the pit. And the revelation of Scripture is of a Father who flies off His porch and down the road, defying the shame of breaking custom and baring His legs by hiking up His robe to run, to the child who should have been cut off.

Reflect on the journey from bondage to bonding you identified above. With that in mind, read the story of the prodigal son: Luke 15:11–32.

The Kezazah ceremony in Jewish custom would cut off any Jew who had lost the Jewish family inheritance to a non-Jew. In this ceremony, the community fills an earthenware jar with burned nuts and corn, and then breaks the jar at the prodigal's feet to symbolize the estrangement, the severed attachment.

The prodigal—you and I—know and dread that we're deserving of the severed attachment, the cutting off from relations forever. Because we've done exactly that—broken faith with our Father; lost the family inheritance. And the prodigal knows the only way now to avoid the Kezazah ceremony of shaming and estranging is to find a way to earn our way back: "Make me a hired servant so I can earn it all back, so I can earn my way."

But, the father has a plan to take all the prodigal's humiliation—all your humiliation, all my humiliation—so there can be complete reconciliation. *Hesed* holds. No created thing can sever us from the love of God who knows that our deepest fear is abandonment and our deepest need is attachment, and He resolves both by being the deepest love who never leaves our side ever.

This is nothing short of apocalyptic, which is what revelation means— *apokalupsis.*

There is never any revelation of God without an apocalypse in us.

Every sacred revelation of God is apocalyptic —a soul reorientation to the Way Himself—who is the only way to find the way.

So, still yourself. Be attentive to God. Arms outstretched in cruciform. And answer: How has God revealed Himself to you today like a burning fire in the dark?

How has God revealed Himself to you *through His Word?*

How has God revealed Himself to you *through His world?*

## SACRED **APPLICATION** FOR TODAY ____ / ____ / ____

Pilgrim, fellow wayfarer, here is the hard, honest truth I've learned firsthand: Keep burying how you feel and you'll end up digging your life a pretty big grave. If you don't speak your fears and questions aloud, and ask God for a revelation of truth, of Himself, of the Way, they only grow louder in your soul. Trying to self-protect is how you begin to self-destruct. Trying to save oneself can be how to *lose* oneself.

Taking care of yourself can take away the joy *God* has in caring for you— and the joy you can only experience *when you let Him love you.*

Instead, pick up your pen, and let the Holy Spirit blaze a way as you ask yourself for fresh revelation to see God—in all the pain, in everything.

Ask God for a personal apocalypse—a literal shaking of your world with a fresh revelation of the WayMaker Himself. Because it's never too late. There is revelation of a blazing pillar of God, the Holy Spirit, waiting in our darkest places. Ask God to reveal Himself to you in His Word and through His world—because He is here, right here. Journal what you hear and feel the Spirit revealing:

_____

_____

_____

_____

_____

_____

_____

_____

_____

_____

_____

_____

_____

_____

_____

_____

_____

_____

_____

_____

_____

_____

# BONUS READING

As you reflect on what you have studied, learned, and journaled from Session 4, you may want to go deeper. Now is a good time to read chapters 12–13 of *WayMaker: Finding the Way to the Life You've Always Dreamed Of.*

# EXAMINE
## to Return to God

## GROUP STUDY

### WELCOME LETTER FROM ANN

*Please ask someone to read this letter aloud as you begin your time together:*

Fellow Wayfarers,

So, it turns out that life isn't about how far you've come, or how far you have to go. It isn't about detours, roadblocks, wrong ways, wildernesses, deep valleys or steep mountains, or the overwhelm that has you between a rock and a hard place. Life is about distance, in relation to God, and living constantly in the direction of God. No measurement in the world matters but the distance between us and God.

Unlikely stories can still become love stories and impossible plotlines can turn on one fierce line of hope. And biblical hope is not about good odds, but about trusting the ways of a good God, our WayMaker, who never stops making His way to us.

So, even when we can't see Him, he's working and making a way to us and we trust the SACRED compass to keep curving us daily toward God through what we have learned together so far: stillness, attentiveness, cruciformity, revelation. And when you feel your heart curving in, that's your sign to turn toward your cleft in the rock, your base, His Word. Let His *hesed*-heart whisper truth to yours, revelation upon apocalyptic, reorienting revelation.

Because it is turning again and again toward healthy attachments that cure soul addictions and turn us in the direction of our soul's true dreams. So, today we turn to the letter "E" in our SACRED compass—E for Examine to return to God.

Your fellow pilgrim on The Way,

# OPEN UP

*Get to know who's on this pilgrimage with you. Each week of group study will begin with a question for the whole group. Though not required, everyone is invited to respond.*

What are you afraid of today?

# VIDEO NOTES AND REFLECTIONS

*View the video segment for Session 5. As you watch the video, use the following outline to note anything that stands out to you, any quotes you want to capture, and any questions or responses you may have.*

**E** is the fifth letter in our SACRED habit—<u>Examine</u> to return to God.

In Exodus 14:30–31, the people of Israel examined how the hand of God had forged an impossible way.

Maybe there's no exodus without an examination.

John Wesley, George Whitefield, Ignatius all made it a daily practice to examine their hearts.

*Examine.* What exactly am I afraid of?

Psalm 56:4—*trust* from the Hebrew, *batach*, literally means "to cling or adhere to something"—or attach to someone.

Our deepest loves drive our deepest fears.

God is safe to trust because we are always soul-safe in Christ!

"There's nothing [anything or anyone] can
do to your soul, your core being"

### MATTHEW 10:28 MSG

It takes time to "fear not," time to trust, but change can take hold.

Examine unspoken fears to deliberately, daily return to God.

# TALK ABOUT IT

*Discuss as many of the following questions as you have time for. Ask for volunteers to read the Bible passages out loud. Invite robust conversation, every voice matters.*

1. What in the video moved you? Is there a quote or a story or an image that stuck most with you? Why?

2. When the Israelites examine what has happened in Exodus 14:30–31, what do they discover? Discuss similar circumstances today in your personal life, or the life of your church, your group, family, etc.

3. We are familiar with reliving our days in the dark hours of 3 a.m. in spirals of regret and shame. Unpack as a group what it means to relive your days as a holy act of examination instead.

4. Honestly share what some of your own life preservers that you cling to in seasons of fear have looked like. Did they actually save you from anything? Examine your "go-to's" as a group and where you end up when you cling to them.

5. Choose a volunteer to read Jeremiah 13:11 aloud. How does this verse make you feel? What changes knowing this?

6. Augustine says, "We fear NOTHING, save (but) to lose what we love."[8] Ann expounds on this idea, that may be at the core: Fear is love of self. Discuss what this might mean and the consequences as a group.

7. Ask a few people if they're willing to share an example from their lives of how God isn't transactional, God is *relational*, making the way to be *with* us *through* pain rather than *keeping us from* pain.

8. Is it easy or difficult for you to identify and admit what you are afraid of? Why? Discuss together.

# CLOSING PRAYER

*Invite a group member to read the paragraphs below aloud. Then make time for everyone to share prayer requests. Close by bringing your prayers to the Father, either silently or out loud, as your group members feel most comfortable.*

A life unexamined ends up unfulfilling. Passing your days with no soul examination is how you fail your only life. Unpack why you're afraid and you send the devil packing.

Friends, all of us are afraid to be found out. But can you be compassionate with your fears, gather them close, and soothe them again with truth: *When you know you are fully known and still fully loved, nothing can still scare you.*

### PRAYER REQUESTS

# PERSONAL APPLICATION

*Here is where we do the personal heart work. You and the WayMaker. Remember, new habits take time to learn. New rhythms require repetition. So, I suggest spreading out this personal study over several days between video sessions. And remember, this isn't about mindless repetition that feels like drudgery. Instead, this is like learning the lyrics to your favorite love song. A daily celebration of the songs the WayMaker sings over you.*

## SACRED **LITURGY** FOR TODAY _____ / _____ / _____

We always begin by applying and practicing the SACRED habits we have learned thus far. So, pick up your pen, friend, and start the day with a liturgy of love; reflect on the first four letters in the acronym SACRED and journal your answers below:

**S:** _____ to _____ God.

What is in my way today and what can I do about it?

**A:** _____ to _____ God.

Who do I say that God is?

Where am I coming from and where am I going to?

What do I want?

**C:** _____ to _____God.

What do I need to surrender today?

**R:** _____ to _____God.

How has God revealed Himself to me today in His Word and through His world?

**And now we turn to the letter "E" in the word SACRED.**

**E: <u>Examine</u> to return to God.** Write it out for yourself below:

**E:** _____ to _____God.

How can we know the Way—without examining the way we are on? E is the fifth letter in our SACRED habit—Examine to return to God.

Like the Israelites in Exodus 14, there are seasons you are going to find yourself between the sea and an overwhelming horde of hard coming at you. In those moments, this SACRED compass is to help keep you in equilibrium with the deepest way of Shalom the way it did for the Israelites:

**S:** In Exodus, after staying <u>still</u> in God, despite the army closing in on them,

**A:** after being <u>**attentive**</u> to God's leading,

**C:** after Moses with hands raised, arms stretched out, in <u>**cruciform**</u> surrender to the will and way of God, the Israelites trusted that God would part the waters,

**R:** after every last man, woman, child, donkey, goat, and chicken walked through the waves, through their own dark uncertainty by the light of a fresh <u>**revelation**</u> of the power and provision of the Father,

**E:** *after all this, what did the Israelites do?*

Read Exodus 14:30–31 ESV. "Thus the Lord saved Israel that day from the hand of the Egyptians, and Israel saw the Egyptians dead on the seashore. Israel saw the great power that the Lord used against the Egyptians, so the people feared the Lord, and they believed in the Lord and in his servant Moses."

**It's worth underlining that second sentence in ink because Israel saw what God did that day.** Israel saw the great power of God, Israel reflected on what God had done, Israel examined how the hand of God had forged an impossible way.

Hadn't Paul implored: "Each one must examine his own work" (Galatians 6:4 NASB)?

Maybe when we relive the day, we see more reasons to believe in the Lord.

Maybe part of the way out of the hard is to examine our hearts.

**Maybe there's no exodus without an examination.**

Maybe it is more than high time for us to slow, still, and pray with all of God's people the words from Lamentations 3:40. Write them below like a prayer from you to God:

## SACRED STUDY FOR TODAY          ___/___/___

Sometimes you don't know you've turned the wrong way till you're down that road a long way. And yet, especially then: Don't doubt that the WayMaker makes wrong ways right. This is the work of a good and kind God. Need, dependence, reliance is what cultivates trust and deepens attachments that make us secure. This is the way of faith.

Trusting the process, trusting the work, trusting the road, trusting the Way, trusting the WayMaker, trusting the kindness of God. Psalm 56:4, says, "In God, whose word I praise, in God I have put my trust" (Psalm 56:4 NASB). The word translated *trust* from the Hebrew, *batach*, literally means "to cling or adhere to something"—or attach to someone.

You are on the way of Jesus only when you need to cling to Jesus the whole way. Life is waves but there is One who says, "Trust Me! Trust Me!"

Do you trust Jesus? Honestly reflect on why or why not. Journal your answers below:

_____

_____

_____

_____

_____

_____

_____

_____

_____

_____

_____

_____

_____

_____

_____

_____

Look up Jeremiah 13:11. Whether you trust God to hold onto you or not, what does God the WayMaker promise to do?

Think about how it makes you feel to know there is a God who promises to literally tie you to Himself in order to keep you safe on the edge of your cliff, your rockface, your sheer drop into the dark unknown. Write or illustrate in the space provided your reaction to that promise:

It takes time to trust, but change can take hold—*if we let God hold us*. Change happens when *identity* changes and our identity is attached to *whom* we are attached, and how they see us, treat us, act toward us. Our God is the God who stays *with* us, exactly so we can see ourselves the way *He* sees us—beloved, cherished, wanted, chosen—because this is what changes our *identity*, and changing one's identity, changes one's whole life.

Healthy attachment cures harmful addictions because when we attach our identity to already being loved, there is nothing more we need.

Turn the pages of God's Word, turn toward Jesus, turn and live, let Him love you through a SACRED love, set apart for Him, and your whole life can turn around.

Put one foot in front of the other—in the right direction—and you can have a new life.

**It's worth writing it down, on your own soul map, on a sticky note, on your hand, across your life:**

**Easy way. Empty life.**

**Hard way. Holy, fulfilling life.**

It's worth sitting long with the words of David, in Psalm 46:1–3, here in the MSG:

God is a safe place to hide,
ready to help when we need him.
We stand fearless at the cliff-edge of doom,
courageous in seastorm and earthquake,
Before the rush and roar of oceans,
the tremors that shift mountains.
Jacob-wrestling God fights for us,
God-of-Angel-Armies protects us.

Take time to look up Psalm 46:1–3 in a couple different translations as well. Meditate on these words. Read and re-read them. Listen to how David, a man after God's own heart, examines his own soul to see where he is in relation to the WayMaker. This examination is how he stays in the Way, knows the Way, is deeply attached to the WayMaker Himself who is the One who will carry him the whole way through. Journal your reactions:

## SACRED **QUESTION** FOR TODAY ____/____/____

To be honest with you, there have been days that I have been terrified of the next cavernous valley, plunging losses, and then skyrocketing challenges, mountain and valley, wave after wave after wave. How in the name of all things good does God work for us and keep us safe when some dreaded phone call detonates, or the shrapnel of shame shreds everything that looks like hope, or the sky lashes round and swallows your dreams whole, or the claw of death guts deep, and how do you stagger forward through the waves? How do you keep going when you are paralyzingly afraid?

So, I keep returning to it every night, to what Jesus asked His disciples to examine in their own hearts, out in the middle of a storm: "Why are you so afraid?" (Mark 4:40)

**Examine. What exactly *are* you afraid of?**

Read Mark 4:35–38. Place yourself in the story, with a furious squall breaking over you.

**Jesus! Wake up!**

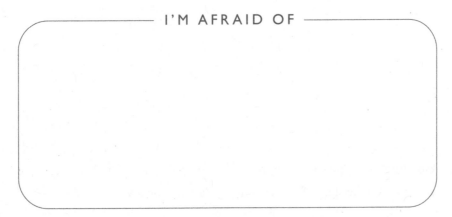

I'M AFRAID OF

Only what you actually name can you actually regulate. Only when you open up, name and express your fears, can the fears begin to ebb, which is why the Word asks us to calm our fears by putting words to them, by bringing them *to* the Word.

"Do not be anxious about anything, but in every situation, by prayer and petition, with thanksgiving, present your requests to God. And the peace of God, which transcends all understanding, will guard your hearts and your minds in Christ Jesus" (Philippians 4:6–7).

"Cast all your anxiety on him because he cares for you" (1 Peter 5:7).

Jesus asks us to examine why we are so afraid because He knows: **Fears can ignite fight-or-flight responses, making our fears masquerade like something else altogether.**

Circle all the masks that your fear wears:

| | | |
|---|---|---|
| Anger | Procrastination | Stuffing |
| Control | Sadness | Hiding |
| Perfectionism | Self-harm | Irritation |

Write down any other masks that you know your fears wear:

God knows no question may matter more than asking ourselves *why* we are so afraid, because: Fear is about losing what we love.

As Augustine points out, "we fear nothing save to lose what we love."[9] Our deepest loves drive our deepest fears. When we want what we want too much, when our love for what we want outsizes our love for God, our fears outsize our living.

I have feared losing what I loved: my hopes, my dreams, my relationships, my reputation, my future, my sense of self. And all the fears are me-centered.

But in practicing the SACRED way, and the daily habit of asking my soul what Jesus asks—"Why are you so afraid?"—I think, examining under all of the layers, that maybe at the core: Fear is love of self. Jesus asks us to explore what we are so afraid of, so we can identify what we are loving more than Him.

What are you afraid of losing, friend? Can you name those things, people, stories you hold gripped so tight in white, terrified knuckles?

Because God really is love, we really are always soul-safe. In Christ *what matters forever, is always forever safe.*

Add your name on the lines in the verse below. Imagine this is what Jesus says to you when you shake Him awake in the middle of your storm:

Dear _____,

"Every detail of your body and soul—even the hairs of your head, _____,

is in my care; nothing of you will be lost. Staying with it—that's what is required. Stay with it to the end, _____.

You won't be sorry, _____; you'll be saved" (Luke 21:17–19 MSG).

## SACRED **APPLICATION** FOR TODAY ____/____/____

Examine—*What are you afraid of today?* Shame dies when our story is shared in safe places, and what place is more safe than on the page, before the Word, to share our fears without shame?

Sharing our fears with our Father regulates our fears.

If Abba Father is not a knot of worry, then why not trust? Let everything loosen into trust, binding your being to His. One. Union.

It turns out you can be about bankrupted, shamed, walked out on, labeled, ghosted, slandered, diagnosed, abandoned, cut off, humiliated, guilty, fired, vilified, charged, destroyed, ruined, devastated, grieved, wrecked, and left for dead in a million ways, and this is the ocean floor, this is at its base:

> When you know you are fully known and still fully loved,
> nothing can still scare you.

God is Love, and love is at rock bottom, love is underneath everything, when everything falls away, and God is with us, and Love marries us.

Fellow pilgrim, fear not. You are known and practicing the habit of daily examination, writing down what you are afraid of, is how you teach yourself how to say it out loud:

**"The worst-case scenario is that all the very worst things happen, and I am still loved."**

Now write that statement out here, with bold and confident strokes:

_____

_____

_____

_____

_____

Then, take your faithful pen again, and journal as you examine your heart to return to God. Start with the question we find Jesus Himself asking those who are trying to follow Him in the Way: What am I afraid of today? And let your pen lead your heart out of fear and back to the soul-safe *hesed*-love of God.

_____

_____

_____

_____

_____

_____

_____

_____

_____

_____

_____

_____

_____

_____

_____

_____

_____

_____

_____

_____

# BONUS READING

As you reflect on what you have studied, learned, and journaled from Session 5, you may want to go deeper. Now is a good time to read chapters 14–15 of *WayMaker: Finding the Way to the Life You've Always Dreamed Of.*

# DOXOLOGY
## to Thank God

## GROUP STUDY

### WELCOME LETTER FROM ANN

*Please ask someone to read this letter aloud as you begin your time together:*

Fellow pilgrims, fellow Wayfarers,

Here we are. Our last day together as pilgrims on the way practicing the daily habit of reorienting our lives on purpose, in relation to the WayMaker, to be in relationship with God. To be attached to God, bonded to God. Because it is only in being bonded to God that we are free from bondage. What an honor to walk with you on the Way.

Friends, there is a Red Sea Road through every impossible and we can learn the language of exodus and we can find the Way through all our hard places.

So, let's slip our journals out again from the bottom of a tote or off a shelf or from next to the sofa and press open the battered pages along with a Bible and a pen, to locate our souls in relation to the WayMaker. Since every relationship is always about location in relation, about distance and orientation. Let us begin our SACRED journaling into Christ's sacred heart because who can actually afford for their soul to lose its very way?

**S:** Stillness to know God. **What always comes first is being still, to know that He is still God, and He turns the obstacle into the miracle.**

**A:** Attentiveness to hear God. **Paying attention to the three questions God asks us,**

*Who do you say that I am?*
*Where are you coming from and where are you going to?*
*What do you want?*

**C:** Cruciformity to surrender to God. **Arms stretched out to God and to people.**

**R:** Revelation to see God through his Word and His World.

**E:** Examine so that you can deliberately, daily keep returning to God, viewing your fear through God's *hesed*-love.

**D:** And finally, today, D for Doxology to thank God.

And friends, no matter the days we feel like we're lost in the wilderness, we can promise to keep stumbling back to wear a habit of gratitude—because thanksgiving gives us a way out of entitlement and judgment and control management, and gratefulness makes for a greater life.

I have been so grateful to keep company with you.

Your fellow pilgrim on The Way,

# OPEN UP

*Get to know who's on this pilgrimage with you. Each week of group study will begin with a question for the whole group. Though not required, everyone is invited to respond.*

What are you grateful for today? Welcome the hard gifts into this exercise of gratitude, too, since all gifts are a grace when given by the WayMaker.

# VIDEO NOTES AND REFLECTIONS

*View the video segment for Session 6. As you watch the video, use the following outline to note anything that stands out to you, any quotes you want to capture, and any questions or responses you may have.*

**D** is the sixth letter in our SACRED habit—**Doxology to thank God.**

Exodus 15:1–2. Because what comes after the exodus is praise and thanksgiving.

Unless I give thanks for the hard gifts, I've miscounted the gifts.

| | | |
|---|---|---|
| Stillness | Cruciformity | Examine |
| Attentiveness | Revelation | |

Doxology. Whatever may come, and no matter what comes, thank God.

The Jews called this Red Sea crossing a *mikveh.*

Exodus 15:20–21 ESV

## TALK ABOUT IT

*Discuss as many of the following questions as you have time for. Ask for volunteers to read the Bible passages out loud. Invite robust conversation, every voice matters.*

1. What in the video moved you? Is there a quote or a story or an image that stuck most with you? Why?

2. When the Israelites had to flee Egypt in the middle of the night taking nothing with them, what is your reaction to learning that they had packed their tambourines?

3. Discuss the parallels between the crossing of the Red Sea, Jesus' own death and resurrection, and the sacrament of baptism.

4. Read Moses and Miriam's song in Exodus 15:1–21. Go around the room and share what lyrics might be in your own love song of exodus if you were singing a song of thanks to God right now. Feel free to get creative; sing them if you like, play a few lines from a favorite song on your phone, or simply share in your own words.

5. The Jews called this Red Sea crossing a *mikveh*—literally a gathering of waters for a spiritual cleansing. Ask a few people if they're willing to share an example from their lives of what they have left behind and washed away as they crossed over their own Red Seas.

6. In a matter of days, the Israelites went from abject terror to astonishing adoration. What has your own journey been like moving through the SACRED liturgy to doxology?

7. Which of the six letters, the six habits of SACRED, has been the most meaningful to you? Share with the group why.

8. Offer members of your group an opportunity to recite the SACRED liturgy one final time, either by memory or reading below:

**S**tillness to know God

**A**ttentiveness to hear God

**C**ruciformity to surrender to God

**R**evelation to see God

**E**xamine to return to God

**D**oxology to thank God

# CLOSING PRAYER

*Invite a group member to read the paragraphs below aloud. Then make time for everyone to share prayer requests. Close by bringing your prayers to the Father, either silently or out loud, as your group members feel most comfortable.*

You can withstand life's rhythms of waves as long as you have your own interior sacred rhythms with God who rocks you safely. The daily habit of a SACRED way of life holds back a storm of worries, a tsunami of fears, by setting the soul apart, through stillness, attentiveness, cruciformity, revelation, examination, and doxology, to let the Spirit soothe the heart with gospel truth.

It's the soul's daily habitual turns that become the soul's eventual destination, and it's the SACRED spiritual disciplines that keep turning the heart to see, to arrive, in the arms of the WayMaker who keeps making the way, His way, to know and be one with Him, soul-safe. His arms are the safest place for all your prayers, friends. Hold nothing back from the God who is always making His way to you.

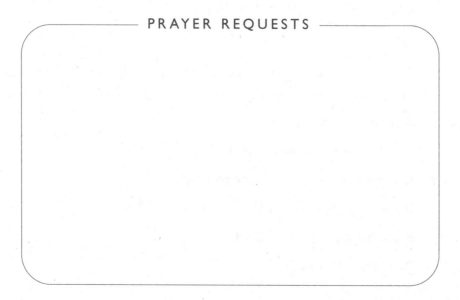

PRAYER REQUESTS

# PERSONAL APPLICATION

*Here is where we do the personal heart work. You and the WayMaker. Remember, new habits take time to learn. New rhythms require repetition. So, I suggest spreading out this personal study over several days between video sessions. And remember, this isn't about mindless repetition that feels like drudgery. Instead, this is like learning the lyrics to your favorite love song. A daily celebration of the songs the WayMaker sings over you.*

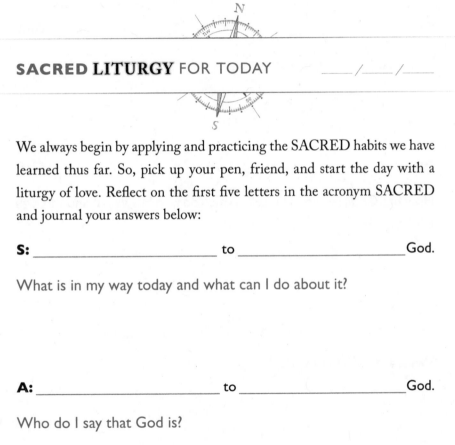

## SACRED **LITURGY** FOR TODAY  _____ / _____ / _____

We always begin by applying and practicing the SACRED habits we have learned thus far. So, pick up your pen, friend, and start the day with a liturgy of love. Reflect on the first five letters in the acronym SACRED and journal your answers below:

**S:** _____ to _____ God.

What is in my way today and what can I do about it?




**A:** _____ to _____ God.

Who do I say that God is?

Where am I coming from and where am I going to?

What do I want?

**C:** _____ to _____God.

What do I need to surrender today?

**R:** _____ to _____God.

How has God revealed Himself to me today in His Word and through His World?

**E:** _____ to _____God.

What am I afraid of today?

**And now we turn to the final letter "D" in the word SACRED.**

**D: <u>Doxology</u> to thank God.** Write it out for yourself below:

**D:** _____ to _____ God.

D is the sixth letter in our SACRED habit—**<u>Doxology</u> to thank God.**

Read Exodus 15:1–2.

Because what comes after the exodus?

Of course. Doxology. Thanksgiving. Praise. I had once been dared by a friend to record one hundred—*hey, how about one thousand gifts*—from the Giver. I radically discovered: If Jesus can give thanks even on the night He was betrayed, then I can give thanks in the midst of anything, and there is always something to be thankful for and thanksgiving always precedes the miracle of more God.

A habit of thankfulness is always our exodus out of bitterness. Christ-exaltation always leads to some kind of exodus. God withholds no good way from us, so there is a way God is making it across the sea of your soul, and if He ceases the hard winds and the storm, you will miss the miracles of many Red Sea Roads. Thanks be to God that: Deserts are not places of despair—deserts are sacred spaces of divine dialogue. Unless you give thanks for the hard gifts, you've miscounted the gifts.

Can you write down ten gifts today, friend? Can you make them all hard gifts? Can you give thanks for those and how they are pointing you to the WayMaker?

1.

2.

3.

4.

5.

6.

7.

8.

9.

10.

## SACRED **STUDY** FOR TODAY ___ / ___ / ___

The exodus through the Red Sea was the Israelites going down, way down under the waters, like descending into a grave, dying to self, submerging their entire beings into God and then rising, resurrected, transformed into a new way of life, a new sacred way of being. As we've studied, the Jews called this Red Sea crossing a *mikveh*—a spiritual cleansing, through water *like a baptism*.

*Mikveh* is derived from the same word as *hope* in Hebrew. Every Red Sea Road is a *mikveh*,[10] a going deeper down and dying in the depths of Christ— to rise, rising into hope! Thanks be to God!

Friend, as you think about the pilgrimage we've been on these last weeks, and your own Red Sea you've been crossing through, what have you left behind, left washed in the water, as you exit on the other side?

*Take some time to reflect and journal about this experience. Consider how you felt as you began this study, what this journey has helped you leave behind, and what fresh hope you are arriving with on the other side.*

_____

_____

_____

_____

_____

_____

_____

_____

_____

_____

_____

_____

_____

_____

_____

_____

_____

_____

_____

After hours of walking through the depths of the sea, Miriam, Aaron, and Moses arrive on the other side where they sing and dance their doxology. There is Miriam with her tambourine because when the Israelites had to flee Egypt in the middle of the night taking nothing with them, it's the women who remembered to grab, of all things, their tambourines, ready for the dance of praise, of thanks.

Then "Miriam the prophetess . . . took a tambourine in her hand, and all the women went out after her with tambourines and dancing. And Miriam sang to them: 'Sing to the LORD'" (Exodus 15:20–21 ESV).

Because even though they were facing a no-way Red Sea—their faith actively trusted God to take care of them through all things and that there is always a way to give thanks to God for His lovingkindness.

To this day, Jews rise and sing Miriam's exact words every morning. There are still women who grab their tambourines when they are between a rock and a Red Sea, trusting that there will be a way through and God is always worthy of thanks, *doxology, doxology, doxology.*

And someday, soon and very soon, we'll be the ones singing the love song of Miriam and Moses with the Song of the Lamb before our wedding supper at the end of time, when we will be His.

Come that last exodus of Revelation, all who keep trust, walking in the Way, will again raise their voices to sing. Read and write down the two parts of the Exodus love song for yourself:

| EXODUS 15: 1–2, 8, 13, 20–21 | REVELATION 15: 2–3 |
| --- | --- |
| After Moses and Miriam crossed through the Red Sea, they led all of Israel to sing this love song to God, recorded for us in Exodus 15. | Come the new and last exodus of Revelation, all who kept trusting in the Way will sing this with all of heaven: |

Like one epic love song in two sacred movements. A love song from one way out, to the forever way in.

Consider ending today's reflection by listening to a favorite song of worship. Play it, sing it, dance it, journal it, illustrate it. Join in however you feel led, as you sing with Moses and Miriam, and all the women who first danced the dance of doxology.

## SACRED **QUESTION** FOR TODAY  ____ / ____ / ____

If Jesus chose to give thanks for the cup of suffering since, out of a cosmos of possibilities, thanksgiving was the preferred weapon to face and fight the dark, do you and I have any better way? When I've been holding on by a thread, what's been holding me together was this looking for a thread of grace still running through everything. And this—this was the going higher up and deeper down into God, the next holy step. Christ-exaltation always leads to some kind of exodus. Any way of life that finds a way through has always had the cadence of doxology.

The dowry for the bride has been paid in full at the cross, by the Lamb whose blood covered the doorposts down in Egypt to make a way for the angel of death to pass over us, by the sacrificed heart of the Lamb who is Jesus, the only One who has ever loved you to death and loved you with His life, back to the realest life.

So, fellow crosser of Red Seas, what are you grateful for today?

## SACRED **APPLICATION** FOR TODAY ____ / ____ / ____

Wayfarers on the Way, pilgrims walking with the Person of Peace, the Red Sea Road is a SACRED way of life! Every step of the way through that Red Sea Road—*stillness, attentiveness, cruciformity, revelation, examination, doxology*—leading out of bondage, out of Egypt, to bonding with God.

Flip back through your journal, friend. Look back through the story, and there it is, right from the beginning, letter by letter, line by line, how the WayMaker, even especially when you were unaware, has always been at work, always making sacred dreams of connection and communion come true.

Look at the compass in your hands, look at what you have written down as all these weeks passed:

**Stillness:** *Be __still__ and live into a tender surrender because the Lord fights His way to me, fights for me in ways I didn't even know I needed.*

**Attentiveness:** *__Attend__ to who I say God is, to where I am in relation to Him, and what I really want.*

**Cruciformity:** *Surrender, arms wide-open, let myself be formed __cruciform__, reaching out to God and people.*

**Revelation:** *See God's Word and His world __revealing__ Himself to me in nothing short of apocalyptic ways.*

**Examine:** *__Examine__ my unspoken fears so that I can deliberately, daily keep returning to God, who casts out all fear.*

**Doxology:** *Hold onto my tambourine when I am between a rock and a Red Sea, trusting that there will be a way through, and God is always worthy of __thanks__.*

Do you see it? A Red Sea Road right there. A way through everything, an exodus emerging directly from Exodus!

A map, a way to a meaningful life. A compass for finding a way *through* that was really about finding a *way of life*, a rule of life.

A new way of thinking.

A new way of being.

The way through happens wherever you stop focusing on how to get out of something and focus on what you can get out of this to become Christlike. Freedom isn't about looking for a way out, but the Way deeper down, the Way to grow into more, to be pressed into the narrow pathway through.

Looking at your page, from this vantage point, you see everything differently, the whole of the story, always making a way into the promised land of union, the WayMaker parting everything to set you apart for deeper intimacy with Him.

Even when you can't see that He's doing *SACRED* work, He's working to part waters to set you apart for a deeper communion with Himself. The WayMaker never, ever, ever, ever stops making a way to be closer to you.

A SACRED way.

Write it down, friend. Today and then again tomorrow and then keep writing it. Every day, take the time to begin your day and end your day by reorienting your soul toward the WayMaker with this SACRED compass:

**S:** _____

_____

**A:** _____

_____

**C:** _____

_____

**R:** _____

_____

**E:** _____

_____

**D:** _____

_____

# BONUS READING

As you reflect on what you have studied, learned, and journaled from Session 6, you may want to go deeper. Now is a good time to read the final chapters, 16–17 of *WayMaker: Finding the Way to the Life You've Always Dreamed Of.* This is the culmination of Ann's honest love story, and her way through to the place she'd only dreamed of—by a way she never expected.

# Endnotes

1 Charles Spurgeon Sermon Collection, *Direction in Dilemma*, https://doi.org/10.5840/augstudies1980114.

2 Dietrich Bonhoeffer, *The Bonhoeffer Reader*, (Minneapolis, MN: Fortress Press) 259.

3 James K.A. Smith, *You Are What You Love: The Spiritual Power of Habit* (Grand Rapids, MI: Brazos Press, 2016).

4 Curt Thompson, *Anatomy of the Soul* (Chicago, IL: Tyndale, 2010) 65–67.

5 Alastair J. Roberts and Andrew Wilson, *Echoes of Exodus: Tracing Themes of Redemption through Scripture* (Wheaton, IL: Crossway, 2018), 125.

6 Paul G. Kuntz, "Augustine: From Homo Erro to Homo Viator," *Augustinian Studies* 11 (1980): 79–89, https://doi.org/10.5840/augstudies1980114.

7 Augustine, quoted in R. Michael Allen, *Reformed Theology* (London: T&T Clark, 2010), 17.

8 St. Thomas Aquinas, *Summa Theologica Part I-II*, (Jazzybee Verlag, 2010).

9 Saint Augustine, quoted in Saint Thomas Aquinas, *Summa Theologica, Part I-II (Pars Prima Secundae)* (Project Gutenberg, 2006), https://gutenberg.org/cache/epub/17897/pg17897.html.

10 (mikveh https://www.chabad.org/theJewishWoman/article_cdo/aid/335957/jewish/Mikvah-The-Art-of-Transition.htm)

# ALSO AVAILABLE FROM ANN VOSKAMP

## A DARE TO LIVE FULL RIGHT WHERE YOU ARE

A five-session, video-based study that leads participants on an exploration of what it means to live life to its fullest through everyday grace—based on the *New York Times* bestselling book.

## OUR BROKENNESS IS MADE WHOLE BY HIS BROKENNESS

The broken way beckons you into more time, more meaning, more authentic relationships. In this six-session video Bible study, Ann leads us through brokenness into a transformed relationship with God through Christ.

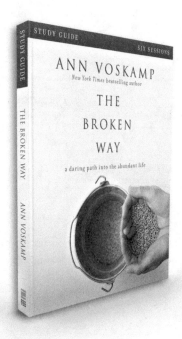

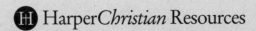

# Companion Book
# to Enrich Your Study Experience

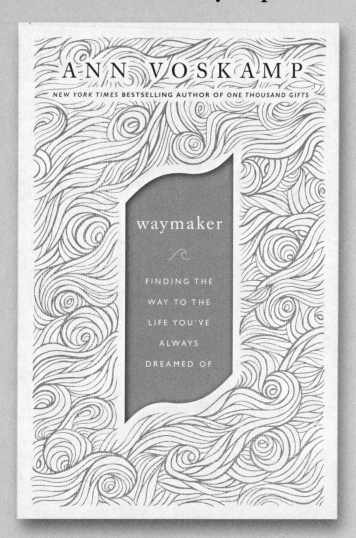

Available wherever books are sold